Terrific Toddlers

All Mine!

by Carol Zeavin, MSEd, MEd
and Rhona Silverbush, JD

illustrated by Jon Davis

Magination Press · Washington, DC · American Psychological Association

American Psychological Association
750 First Street NE
Washington, DC 20002

With gratitude to my inspiring teachers and mentors at Bank Street, Rockefeller, and Barnard—*CZ*
Dedicated to the inspiration for this series, with infinite love—*RS*
For Laura and Greta—*JD*

Magination Press is a registered trademark of the American Psychological Association.
Order books here: www.apa.org/pubs/magination or 1-800-374-2721

Book design by Gwen Grafft
Printed by Worzalla, Stevens Point, WI

Library of Congress Cataloging-in-Publication Data
Names: Zeavin, Carol, author. | Silverbush, Rhona, 1967 – author. | Davis,
    Jon, 1969 – illustrator.
Title: All mine! / by Carol Zeavin, MSEd, MEd, and Rhona Silverbush, JD ;
    illustrated by Jon Davis.
Description: Washington, DC : Magination Press, [2018] | Series: Terrific toddlers
Identifiers: LCCN 2017038179| ISBN 9781433828775 (hardcover) |
    ISBN 1433828774 (hardcover)
Subjects: LCSH: Sharing in children—Juvenile literature. | Sharing—
    Juvenile literature.
Classification: LCC BF723.S428 Z43 2018 | DDC 177/.1—dc23 LC record
    available at https://lccn.loc.gov/2017038179

Manufactured in the United States of America
10 9 8 7 6 5 4 3 2 1

Sometimes we need toys all to ourselves!
And for now, that's OK.

Kai is in the dress-up corner.
He is wearing a very fancy hat.
He looks good!

Ava wants the hat.
She grabs it! Kai shrieks!

The teacher says, "Kai, you were still using that hat. Ava, I can't let you grab Kai's hat. But here's a sparkly necklace."

Ava wants the sparkly necklace.
But she wants the fancy hat, too.
"Kai, tell Ava, 'I'm still using it,'"
the teacher says.

Kai says, "I using it!"

Ava is now in
the play kitchen.
She is putting a carrot
on a plate. Yummy!

JoJo wants Ava's carrot.
JoJo grabs one end of the carrot.
Ava holds tight to the other end.
They both shriek!

Here comes the teacher to help.
"I see you both want that carrot. But Ava's not done yet.
JoJo, here's the asparagus—let's make a stew with Ava."

JoJo does not want to make stew.
She still wants the carrot.
"Ava, tell JoJo, 'You can have it
when I'm done,'" the teacher says.

Ava says, "When I done!"

Later, JoJo is at the art table
drawing with crayons.
Red! Blue! Yellow! Big lines!
Circles! Scribbles!

Kai wants to draw with crayons, too.
He reaches for a crayon.
JoJo hugs the basket tightly.

First the teacher
talks to JoJo. "JoJo,
I see you need all
the crayons right now."

Then she talks to Kai.
"It's hard when you
don't get a crayon, but
JoJo isn't ready yet.
Here are some markers
while you're waiting."
She says, "JoJo, tell Kai,
'they're all mine.'"

JoJo looks at Kai.
The teacher smiles at JoJo.

JoJo says, "ALL MINE!"

And for now, that's OK.

Note to Parents and Caregivers

"*What?!*" you're thinking. "Not even one crayon? How could that teacher condone JoJo's utterly selfish behavior?!" We understand. Naturally, you want your child to grow up to be a generous-spirited person. And so do we! However, what looks like selfishness is actually your toddler learning to master not only the concept of ownership but first and foremost that of self, and of self as separated from others and objects.

Your toddler is part-way between baby and child. A baby has no idea that she is a person separate from those around her. Your young toddler is just starting to figure this out, and, believe it or not, total, categorical ownership of objects is a crucial element in establishing the sense of self. "I have, therefore I am" is the watchword for toddlerhood. If it looks selfish, that's exactly the developmental point. Identity, autonomy, boundaries between self and others, all have their foundations in toddlers mastering the concept of ownership.

Furthermore, your toddler does not yet have a firm enough grasp of her world to understand that if she gives something up, she'll ever get it back.

"Sharing" is simply not a concept that a young toddler can grasp...yet. It may seem counterintuitive, but in fact, encouraging full ownership, as the teacher does for JoJo in *All Mine!*, can actually hasten the development of generosity, since allowing the toddler to fully be in this phase of development hastens her mastery of the lessons about self that it provides.

It is not until at least age three—when young children are developmentally ready to want acceptance from peers and have a firm understanding of the concept of self—that they can begin to want to share.

Thus, allowing full ownership—a stage we call "pre-turn-taking/pre-sharing"—must precede both turn-taking and then sharing.

More and more early childhood centers are attuned to recent brain development research and are allowing for the natural evolution of ownership to turn-taking to, ultimately, sharing behaviors. They understand, further, that there will be tears and tantrums from one child or the other whether they foist "sharing" on toddlers or acknowledge the toddlers' need for ownership—these are toddlers, after all! At least by doing the latter, the toddlers in their care are able to move forward developmentally, with a sense of security and the feeling that they are understood along the way.

So the bottom line is: the more fully you accept your toddlers' temporary need for items to be "all mine," the sooner they will joyfully and readily pass through this phase...and the next...and can emerge as the generous people you hope they will become.

Carol Zeavin holds master's degrees in education and special education from Bank Street College, worked with infants and toddlers for nearly a decade as head teacher at Rockefeller University's Child and Family Center and Barnard's Toddler Development Center, and worked at Y.A.I. and Theracare. She lives in New York, NY.

Rhona Silverbush studied psychology and theater at Brandeis University and law at Boston College Law School. She represented refugees and has written and co-written several books, including a guide to acting Shakespeare. She currently coaches actors, writes, tutors, and consults for families of children and teens with learning differences and special needs. She lives in New York, NY.

Jon Davis is an award-winning illustrator of more than 70 books. He lives in England.